Social Media
and
Depression

How to be Healthy and Happy
in the Digital Age

GREGORY L. JANTZ, PHD
WITH KEITH WALL

AspirePress

AspirePress

Social Media and Depression:
How to be Healthy and Happy in the Digital Age
© 2021 Gregory L. Jantz
Published by Aspire Press
An imprint of Hendrickson Publishing Group
Rose Publishing, LLC
P.O. Box 3473
Peabody, Massachusetts 01961-3473 USA
www.HendricksonPublishingGroup.com

ISBN 978-162862-987-3

Printed in the United States of America
010421VP

Contents

Is Social Media *a* Positive *or* Negative Force?

If you listen to some voices out there, social media is the Dark Side of the Force—period. According to that view, social media platforms are responsible for everything from privacy trespasses to mind control—and are detrimental to people who use them. They argue that we should all delete every app from our devices and never look back.

Well, not so fast. That's like saying we should throw away our car keys and never drive again because automobiles can be dangerous. Yes, crashes happen, but modern transportation delivers a wide range of benefits that offset the risks—if you take care to drive responsibly.

The same can be said of social media use. Here are some ways it can make life better:

- Consistent connection with friends and family

- Reduced feelings of isolation among the elderly

- Opportunities to promote a small business or organization

- Raising awareness and funds to support a cause that's important to you

- Tools for spreading vital information to the community during an emergency

Nevertheless, these positives do not mean that adverse effects don't exist or shouldn't be taken seriously. It's true that a growing body of research makes it more clear each year that social media use does indeed have a dark side—including the elevated risk of depression and anxiety. But, keep in mind that avoiding negative outcomes is not the only reason to educate ourselves about the pitfalls and learn to avoid them. Preserving the benefits of responsible social media engagement is also a payoff worth pursuing.

With that in mind, the dangers posed by excessive or imbalanced use of social media include:

- Increased anxiety and depression

- Distorted sense of identity

- Connection addiction and FOMO—the Fear of Missing Out

- Lower self-esteem and comparison anxiety

- A false sense of intimacy

- Cyberbullying

- Physical stagnation

- Decreased happiness and satisfaction in life

This book will reveal where those pitfalls most commonly lie when using social media, show you how to recognize when they begin to take a toll on your mental health, and offer proven steps you can take to manage the risks and make the technology work for you, not the other way around.

In the pages ahead, I'll share the latest research into the relationship between social media and mental health. Your part will be to honestly assess your own vulnerabilities and to choose best practices to minimize them. Together, I'm confident we can all stay safe and sound in the online world.

CHAPTER 1

From Zero *to* Everywhere

How Social Media Took the World by Storm

Ask some scholars about the origin of social media, and they'll point all the way back to May 24, 1844. That's the day Samuel Morse sent the first telegraph over the wires from the US Capitol to a railroad station in Baltimore, Maryland.

Of all the content he could have conveyed, Morse chose to transmit a Bible verse from the Old Testament: "What hath God wrought?" More than likely he was simply in awe of the invention … or perhaps he'd had a premonition of the double-edged sword that electronic communication would one day become.

Nearly a century and a half later, the telegraph's offspring—the landline telephone—was still the only "social medium" in widespread use. It allowed people to stay in touch with friends and family, keep up on community gossip, get help in case of an emergency, and arrange appointments to actually socialize with others. People old enough to remember being confined to one location in the house while talking on the phone—because it was fixed to the wall or attached by a short cable—are rightly astonished at the immense speed and magnitude of change in the past two decades alone.

And yet, hardly anyone considered the telephone to be a source of mental health disorders. As we progress through this book, we'll seek to answer the question: What makes digital communication in general—and social media in particular—so much more likely to be associated with adverse health outcomes than other historic forms?

From Zero *to* Everywhere *in* No Time

The first modern, Internet-based social media platform was called SixDegrees, in reference to the idea that there are only "six degrees of separation" between any two people in a community, making the social web far smaller than most people imagine. Founded in 1997, the group eventually boasted a million registered users who could create profiles and "friend" one another.

That's ancient history now. Since then, the one has become many:

- 1999—LiveJournal
- 2002—Friendster
- 2003—LinkedIn
- 2003—Myspace
- 2004—Gmail
- 2004—Facebook
- 2005—YouTube
- 2009—WhatsApp
- 2010—Twitter
- 2010—Instagram
- 2011—Snapchat
- 2017—TikTok

… and many other niche platforms too numerous to list. But in that short period of time, usage has now grown to breathtaking proportions.

Without question, social media platforms have become a dominant presence in the world, affecting everything from how we form and maintain relationships to how we elect our leaders. Digital communication now shapes and conveys our values and our sense of self and others. More importantly, the physical and mental demands of sustained social media engagement are something entirely new in human history—with sometimes challenging consequences.

Can Social Media Use Cause Depression?

That turns out to be a complicated question. The simplest answer is—probably, but we don't know for sure. That may sound like a less-than-definitive response, and there's a reason: Social media is a relatively new phenomenon, and a growing (but also relatively new) body of research is emerging and slowly providing data and answers.

Here's a more definitive response: Enough credible research already exists to know that social media does indeed *contribute* to depression.

At the heart of this question about social media and depression is a "chicken-or-the-egg" conundrum that is difficult, if not impossible, to resolve. It's true that researchers have seen an increase in depression-like symptoms among some users of social media. But did their online activity *cause* their feelings of depression, or simply amplify a condition that was already there? Put more directly, does use of social media cause depression, or do depression-prone people gravitate toward riskier social media use? Clear answers are still emerging.[1]

But another way to look at this is to ask: Does it matter? Whether social media causes depression or only aggravates it, the people who suffer increased symptoms of mental health distress deserve a chance to better understand the problem and protect themselves from it. This is particularly true among children and teenagers, who are the largest segment of the population engaged in frequent social media networking. Since young people already experience elevated mental and emotional stresses associated with adolescence, helping them navigate the online world safely is paramount. The stakes can literally be a matter of life and death.

SOCIAL MEDIA PLATFORMS HAVE BECOME A DOMINANT PRESENCE IN THE WORLD, AFFECTING EVERYTHING FROM HOW WE FORM AND MAINTAIN RELATIONSHIPS TO HOW WE ELECT OUR LEADERS.

A Slippery Slope

Katrina described herself as one of her high school's "invisibles." She considered herself to be "cute but not pretty," good in school but not brilliant, and not a loner but mostly overlooked by her peers. Her only two friends were also invisible—that is, they were the kind of kids who only stood out at roll call and barely even then.

Then, for her seventeenth birthday, Katrina's parents gave her a smartphone—and she discovered social media. At first, she was elated, believing the device to be her ticket to finally getting noticed by her peers. Katrina knew she had more to offer than anyone had ever given her credit for. She was sure that in the free flow of online profiles, photos, clever videos, and life status updates, everyone could be equally visible.

SOCIAL MEDIA DOES INDEED *CONTRIBUTE* TO DEPRESSION.

The first thing Katrina's parents noticed was how much less time she spent engaged with the family routine at home. She had always been close with her siblings but suddenly refused any invitation to do things together. She began skipping family activities and meals. Instead, she devoted more and more time to engagement with multiple social networking channels, creating and maintaining her online "presence."

Her friends, who were already on social media themselves, tried to tell Katrina they hardly recognized the digital persona she presented, but she wouldn't listen. This became a rift that isolated her from them as well.

"I just thought they were jealous," she told me. "I was finally getting 'liked,' and nothing else mattered."

Early on, Katrina was thrilled at how many people "followed" her online and "liked" what she posted. She spent large amounts of time looking at what others posted, taking note of which things got the most positive feedback. She used that insight to create similar content herself, sometimes imitating other girls in posts that focused on physical appearance. She watched hours of makeup tutorials and fashion videos. Gradually, her "real life" persona started to match the one she presented online. Boys began leaving suggestive messages on her pages—some of them not bothering to be at all subtle.

"They came right out and asked me for sex," she said. "I thought they were gross, but a part of me liked the attention." Eventually, one of the boys asked Katrina to send him a partially nude photo—because "that's what everyone does." He sent her a pornographic photo of himself to prove it. She reluctantly agreed.

A week later, the photo of Katrina appeared on a social media site widely used by her school peers—and her life became a living hell. She was bombarded by lewd comments from both boys and girls.

In a tragic irony, Katrina's social isolation was now very advanced. She spent all her time monitoring her pages, even sleeping with her phone in bed, set to notify her of new comments at all hours. She tried to combat the negative attention with defensive comments of her own, but she was outmatched and outgunned.

"I should have asked for help, but I was too ashamed," she recalls.

Katrina developed symptoms of severe depression and anxiety. She stopped eating well, slept very little, and took a nosedive academically. In a moment when she was particularly depleted, one of her more vocal detractors posted a message that read, "If I had to wake up being you every day, I'd want to off myself." It was as if someone removed the last piece in Katrina's swaying tower of mental Jenga blocks—and her whole life came crashing down.

Looking back, Katrina remembers feeling almost relieved at the idea that her torment could actually end. The next morning, she skipped school and ingested a whole bottle of acetaminophen tablets. Had her mother not returned home to fetch her forgotten cell phone, Katrina might well have died.

She was a lucky one. Too many young people like her succeed in taking their own lives after getting trapped in distorted thinking that's at least enabled, if not outright fueled, by social media exposure.

"It was like living in a horror movie where the monsters can get to you 24/7," Katrina said. "I knew it was hurting me. I just couldn't turn it off."

A Technology Trap

Look again at that last sentence—"I just couldn't turn it off"—and you'll see a clue to what gives social media such negative potential for some people: It can be powerfully *addictive*. But not uniquely so. In fact, social media is just one facet of a much larger force in modern life—our fascination with digital media in general.

While technology addiction is not yet recognized as a mental disorder in the *Diagnostic and Statistical Manual of Mental Disorders*, researchers are exploring the possibility that spending too much time interacting with our electronic devices can lead to negative mental health consequences that are similar to other forms of addiction. As psychologist and technology researcher Shainna Ali points out:

> [The] general use of the TV for binge-watching your favorite series, the use of your computer for writing reports and checking emails, and the use of your cellphone for scrolling social applications (e.g., Instagram, Twitter, Snapchat, LinkedIn) could all pave the path to a potential problem.[2]

That "problem" may have far reaching implications, not just for personal health and well-being, but also for society as a whole.

In the 1970s, researchers and critics began to sound the alarm about what happens when people—particularly children—spend too much time watching television. In 1985, a full decade before the Internet entered common life, Neil Postman wrote *Amusing Ourselves to Death: Public Discourse in the Age of Show Business*. His warning might have been written today, and with even more urgency:

> When a population becomes distracted by trivia, when cultural life is redefined as a perpetual round of entertainments, when serious public

conversation becomes a form of baby-talk, when, in short, a people become an audience, and their public business a vaudeville act, then a nation finds itself at risk; culture-death is a clear possibility.[3]

This is a fair description of a lot of the content appearing on digital media platforms today—including social media, but also encompassing comment streams on news sites, blogs, sponsored "articles" that purport to be news, pervasive pornography, influencer YouTube shows, and endless memes that indeed reduce conversation to "baby-talk" levels of simplicity. This is at least a part of the troubled cultural environment that Katrina entered—along with millions of others like her—when she engaged in social media.

> SPENDING TOO MUCH TIME INTERACTING WITH OUR ELECTRONIC DEVICES CAN LEAD TO NEGATIVE MENTAL HEALTH CONSEQUENCES THAT ARE SIMILAR TO OTHER FORMS OF ADDICTION.

When Postman wrote those words, cable television was in its infancy. CNN, the first 24/7 broadcast news service, was barely five years old. It's no exaggeration to say that over the following decades we not only saw an exponential increase in digital programming of all kinds, but also in the number of platforms that deliver it without ceasing.

Nor is it hyperbole to suggest that many of us, like Katrina, simply "can't turn it off." Consider these figures:

- More than 2 billion people log into YouTube every month.

- Those users watch over a billion hours of video every day.

- More than 70 percent of that time is spent on mobile devices.[4]

- Viewers watch 140 million hours of programming on Netflix every day.[5]

- Among American young people, 48 percent report being online "almost constantly," while another 46 percent say they go online "multiple times a day."[6]

But Is All *of* This Really *a* Problem?

The World Health Organization (WHO) thinks the answer is *yes*. In a 2014 report following a global summit on "Public Health Implications of Excessive Use of the Internet, Computers, Smartphones and Similar Electronic Devices," WHO experts concluded:

> [The] rapidly increasing use of the Internet and electronic devices with enormous benefits for societies and different domains of a person's life

can also result in health consequences which are of concern from a public health perspective. The observed and documented negative health and psychosocial consequences include a range of health conditions that share signs and symptoms with disorders such as gambling disorder and substance use disorders.[7]

The following list of potential negative consequences to public health and well-being is drawn from the report.

- **SEDENTARY LIFESTYLE:** Excessive screen time—and the associated poor diet, decreased sleep time, and insufficient physical fitness—is linked to obesity and being overweight, as well as other potential health risks.

- **VISION:** Prolonged use of devices with screens may potentially lead to eye and visual symptoms like ocular discomfort, eyestrain, dry eye, headache, blurred vision, and even double vision.

- **MUSCULOSKELETAL PROBLEMS:** Extended use of those devices in a fixed posture can cause or exacerbate musculature and skeletal symptoms.

- **SOCIAL DEVELOPMENT:** Spending too much time online and using modern electronic devices may cause social withdrawal and/or hinder social skill development—through decreased face-to-face interaction and unreal social interactions online.

HEARING: Electronic devices with audio entertainment functions can typically generate harmful levels of sound, which can be linked to permanent hearing damage.

INJURIES AND ACCIDENTS: Mobile electronic devices, such as smartphones, are commonly used while doing other tasks, which may make the user more prone to injuries and accidents.

INFECTIONS: Insufficient hygiene precautions and sharing of mobile devices such as smartphones may enable the spread of pathogens and infectious diseases.

CYBERBULLYING: Modern technologies and the Internet enable a new type of bullying which is associated with a range of serious psychosocial consequences.

RISKY SEXUAL BEHAVIORS: Sexualized online content may increase risky sexual behavior.

SLEEP DEPRIVATION: Excessive use of electronic devices often deprives people of adequate sleep, which affects growth and development in children and adolescents.

- **AGGRESSIVE BEHAVIORS:** Violent content of videos and online games may have adverse effects on the behavior of children, adolescents, and adults.

- **OTHER SOCIAL AND PSYCHOLOGICAL PROBLEMS:** Excessive use of the Internet and electronic devices can be associated with a range of social and psychological problems such as poor psychological well-being, poor self-confidence, family problems, marital breakdown, and reduced work and academic performance.

A growing body of research in the years since the report was written strongly underscores the phrase "poor psychological well-being" in that final bullet point— particularly where social media use is concerned. Again, psychologists warn against ignoring potential positive effects as we take stock of what can go wrong, but for some people at least, these dangers are very real.

Rather than suggesting that at-risk people simply avoid social media altogether, one recent study concluded that "individuals with [Major Depressive Disorder] or depressive symptoms should develop an awareness of the specific negative social media behaviors that may exacerbate their depressive symptoms and acquire an understanding of positive social media behaviors that may reduce those symptoms."[8]

That is precisely what this book aims to do—help you "acquire an understanding" of both positive and negative social media behaviors, so you can avoid the pitfalls that imbalanced social media use can have on your mental health.

But Is Social Media *a* Problem *for Me?*

To help answer that important question, let's begin with a self-assessment tool to help you see where you stand. Be brutally honest with your responses.

☐ Do you begin your day by "checking in" on your social media channels?

☐ Do you sleep with your phone or device in bed with you?

☐ Does late-night engagement with social media cause you to sleep less than is recommended?

☐ Do you feel agitated if separated from your device?

☐ Do you feel agitated when unable to access your social media pages for some reason?

☐ Do you "check in" while doing other things, such as having dinner, driving, or talking with someone in person?

- [ ] Is social media your main form of communication and interaction with others?

- [ ] Do you often interrupt what you are doing in order to take a picture of it to post on social media?

- [ ] Do you ever ignore other responsibilities while engaged with social media?

- [ ] Do you sometimes forget to eat while engaged with social media?

- [ ] Do you ever feel surprised at how much time has elapsed while you were engaged with social media?

- [ ] Do you use social media as a way to "tune out" personal problems?

- [ ] Have you ever resolved to reduce your use of social media without success?

- [ ] When you make a post, do you pay close attention to how others interact with it?

- [ ] Does your mood ever seem to depend on that interaction?

- [ ] Do you often have difficulty focusing on other activities?

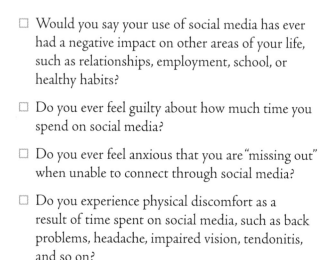

☐ Would you say your use of social media has ever had a negative impact on other areas of your life, such as relationships, employment, school, or healthy habits?

☐ Do you ever feel guilty about how much time you spend on social media?

☐ Do you ever feel anxious that you are "missing out" when unable to connect through social media?

☐ Do you experience physical discomfort as a result of time spent on social media, such as back problems, headache, impaired vision, tendonitis, and so on?

There is no scientific formula to evaluate your answers. Suffice it to say that if you answered *yes* to even a few of these questions, you may be at higher risk of addiction—and the adverse mental health consequences that come with it. By contrast, this checklist may reveal that you have kept your social media use in balance and enjoy the positive benefits it has to offer.

The truth is, engagement with digital media has an effect on the human brain that is very much like other mood-altering substances. In the next chapter, we'll explore how that works and what you can do to manage the experience safely.

A SNAPSHOT OF SOCIAL MEDIA USE

Social media has changed the way we live our lives—from the way we get our news to the way we interact with our loved ones. Since 2004, social media has been growing exponentially, and it likely has not yet reached the peak of its popularity.

Just how popular has social media become in the United States and around the world? Consider these statistics:

- Daily active social media users: 3.5 billion people. This equates to about 45 percent of the world population.[9]

- Facebook remains the most widely used social media platform, with more than 2.3 billion active monthly users. Roughly two-thirds (68 percent) of US adults are Facebook users.[10]

- YouTube boasts 1.9 billion users, followed by Instagram at 1 billion.[11]

- In wealthy countries, average social media usage among young people (ages 16–24) reached almost 90 percent.[12]

- In the US, the average adult spends about six hours a day engaged with online media, including social media sites.[13]

- For many users, social media is part of their daily routine. Roughly three-quarters of Facebook users—and around six-in-ten Instagram users—visit these sites at least once a day.[14]

WHAT SCIENTIFIC STUDIES ARE REVEALING

From a *CBS News* report:

A new review of several studies shows the potentially harmful impact of social media use on teenagers. It confirms what many parents have long feared.

The results in the Canadian Medical Association Journal finds social media use is linked to mental distress, self-harm and suicide. More than two hours of social media use a day is associated with higher rates of depression and suicidal thoughts in girls.

In one study, girls reported feeling negative after 10 minutes of browsing Facebook. The more time, the greater the risk.[15]

From a study highlight in *Science Direct*:

Compared to those who used 0-2 social media platforms, participants who used 7-11 social media platforms had substantially higher odds of having increased levels of both depression and anxiety symptoms. Associations were linear and robust to all sensitivity analyses.

Use of multiple social media platforms is independently associated with symptoms of depression and anxiety, even when controlling overall time spent on social media. These associations are strong enough that it may be valuable for clinicians to ask individuals with depression and anxiety about multiple platform use and to counsel regarding this potential contributing factor.[16]

Findings from a study in the *Journal of Depression and Anxiety.*

A new study found a link between high usage of social media sites and increased depression. The research, funded by the U.S. National Institutes of Health (NIH), involved nearly 1,800 individuals and tracked their usage of 11 well-known social media platforms, including Facebook, Snapchat, Instagram, and others.

The researchers found that the participants checked into social media an average of 30 times per week for just over an hour per day. Testing revealed that approximately one-quarter of the participants were at a high risk of depression. When social media and depression are compared, it was determined that those who used social media the most were about 2.7 times more likely to be depressed than participants who used social media the least.[17]

CHAPTER 2

A Digital Drug

How Social Media Is Like a Mood-altering Drug

To begin, let's be clear about the important, and possibly misleading, phrase *social media addiction*. These days, words have a way of taking on common definitions in the media and in casual conversation, and that's okay. We can understand an issue in general without the need for clinical precision.

But once we begin speaking of the potential for serious mental health ramifications—and open the door to possible stigma or folk medicine "diagnoses"— it's important to be sure our judgments account for the current thinking among mental health professionals, not just (ironically) accepting what we see online.

Consider that the *Diagnostic and Statistical Manual of Mental Health Disorders, Fifth Edition* (DSM-5)—the comprehensive guide issued by the American Psychiatric Association and used by all mental health caregivers to assess and diagnose patients—does not include social media addiction as a recognized disorder. A clue as to why is found in the fact that the only behavioral addiction disorder listed in DSM-5 is gambling. Though other things are commonly thought of as addictive—pornography, shopping, food, Internet usage, and so on—none are considered to be officially diagnosable disorders. The missing element for authors of the guide appears to be a person's persistent use despite suffering clear harm as a result. In the case of social media, its use provides measurable benefits as well as potential downsides, muddying the waters even further.

By contrast, the DSM-5 includes extensive guidance on conditions that fall under the heading of "substance abuse disorders." Studying the criteria for diagnosing those patients gives us a way to judge where social media use stacks up in the real world, not just in the restrictive realm of professional mental health treatment.

Take a look at the following eleven behaviors grouped into four categories.[18] As you read, be aware that the presence of any two items over a period of twelve months is enough to justify a substance abuse disorder diagnosis.

Impaired Control	(1) Taking more or for longer than intended
	(2) Unsuccessful efforts to stop or cut down use
	(3) Spending a great deal of time obtaining, using, or recovering from use
	(4) Craving for substance
Social Impairment	(5) Failure to fulfill major obligations due to use
	(6) Continued use despite problems caused or exacerbated by use
	(7) Important activities given up or reduced because of substance use
Risky Use	(8) Recurrent use in hazardous situations
	(9) Continued use despite physical or psychological problems that are caused or exacerbated by substance use
Pharmacologic Dependence	(10) Tolerance to effects of the substance
	(11) Withdrawal symptoms when not using or using less

It's not hard to see that most—if not all—of the items on this list could easily describe the effects of excessive social media use for many people. Indeed, numerous recent studies have started to collect evidence to back that up.

One such report states:

> There is a growing scientific evidence base to suggest excessive use [of social media sites] may lead to symptoms traditionally associated with substance-related addictions. These symptoms have been described as salience, mood modification, tolerance, withdrawal, relapse, and conflict with regards to behavioral addictions, and have been validated in the context of the Internet addiction components model.[19]

In other words, it is becoming increasingly clear that, for some people, excessive use of social media is a real problem—enough so that it may eventually be included in professional treatment guidelines. However, we don't have to wait for the publication of DSM-6 before taking the issue seriously and searching for treatment strategies that work to alleviate suffering and restore well-being to those who are affected.

Brain Games

The science of addiction is far from clear, but one thing can be said with certainty: At the heart of the matter is how the brain perceives and processes psychological "reward." In fact, scientists have long understood the neurochemical "payoff" we get anytime something occurs to make us feel good. It's delivered by a pleasure-producing compound called dopamine that's manufactured naturally by the body. In this respect, it turns out that excessive social media use doesn't simply mimic the effects of a substance abuse disorder; both have the power to directly influence how the brain responds to dopamine "hits"—and what we will do to get another. A Harvard publication called "Dopamine, Smartphones, and You" sums it up like this:

> Dopamine is a chemical produced by our brains that plays a starring role in motivating behavior. It gets released when we take a bite of delicious food, when we have sex, after we exercise, and, importantly, when we have successful social interactions. In an evolutionary context, it rewards us for beneficial behaviors and motivates us to repeat them.[20]

The problem arises when we begin to think of a "beneficial behavior" as *anything* that makes us feel good by triggering a release of dopamine, regardless of what clearly negative consequences come along with it.

"A Virtually Unlimited Supply"

Here's where social media enters the picture. "Successful social interactions"—those that produce a sense of

belonging and holding valued status among others—
are what we all seek when we first log on to a social
networking site and create a profile.

In times past, that meant literally
joining a group, arranging your
schedule to be physically present
for activities, and interacting
with flesh-and-blood people. The
arrangement was, by its very nature,
limited in time and space. That
meant the potential for these kinds
of social interactions to trigger a
person's neurochemical reward
system was also limited. Constant
access to one another through
open channels of communication
was generally not possible. While
we might have wanted to re-create
related dopamine-producing expe-

riences again and again, we simply weren't readily able
to do so.

Technology has changed all that. The above article
continues the comparison between social media and
substance use:

Although not as intense as a hit of cocaine,
positive social stimuli will similarly result in a

release of dopamine, reinforcing whatever behavior preceded it. ... Smartphones have provided us with a virtually unlimited supply of social stimuli, both positive and negative. Every notification, whether it's a text message, a "like" on Instagram, or a Facebook notification, has the potential to be a positive social stimulus and dopamine influx.[21]

Long gone are the days when "real life" was mostly an analog experience—that is, unmediated by technology. Today, most people arrange their lives as if the digital world is more real than anything happening in a physical sense—and keep their devices close and set to notify them of every new online "event." Thirty years ago, even the person suffering a gambling addiction generally had to seek out a casino and load quarters into slot machines, possibly for hours, before hitting the (dopamine) jackpot.

> **TODAY, MOST PEOPLE ARRANGE THEIR LIVES AS IF THE DIGITAL WORLD IS MORE REAL THAN ANYTHING HAPPENING IN A PHYSICAL SENSE.**

Today, for users of social media, that payoff comes in the form of every "like" or share or favorable comment on our posts. Even the comments we leave on the posts of others can get a "thumbs up" from our online "friends" and become a "successful social interaction"—hundreds of times a day. Anywhere, anytime.

Unintended Consequences? *Not Exactly.*

All the above is simply a matter of biology. Human beings are endowed with neurochemicals like dopamine for very good reasons. For instance, it plays a huge roll in romantic attraction and bonding. We couldn't turn it off even if we wanted to—in spite of the role it plays in addiction.

This reality is not lost on the people who design and operate social media platforms. In fact, they count on it. Nearly all social media sites are free for users. They make their money by placing advertisements where people can see them, often in the form of sponsored posts that look a lot like yours. The coveted goal for online marketers is *engagement*—getting you to follow those links and respond to their calls to action, buying whatever it is they are selling.

The math is simple: The longer you stay online—because you are being constantly "rewarded" for being there—the more likely you are to see and engage with an advertisement. Owners of social media sites don't benefit directly from all those "likes" and affirming emojis. Just like TV programmers or magazine designers, their motive for keeping you happy is to keep your attention available to their marketing clients.

However, here's the problem: The potential for experiencing negative mental health outcomes while engaged with social media is very much a function of *time*. More time online is good for marketers, but increasingly bad for users. Behind the scenes, programmers employ sophisticated algorithms to steer users to any content that will keep them enthralled and plugged in. If you spend time today reading negative stories about frightening world events, tomorrow your feed will include more of the same and show you more posts by "friends" who seem to share your concerns. This effectively fits you with blinders, reinforcing your natural biases—all for the purpose of extending your stay online.

MORE TIME ONLINE IS GOOD FOR MARKETERS, BUT INCREASINGLY BAD FOR USERS.

In 2017, former Facebook Vice President of User Growth, Chamath Palihapitiya, made a stunning admission during an interview at Stanford University:

> The short-term, dopamine-driven feedback loops that we have created are destroying how society

works. No civil discourse. No cooperation. Misinformation. Mistruth. And it's not an American problem. This is not about Russian ads. This is a global problem. So we are in a really bad state of affairs right now, in my opinion. ... I feel tremendous guilt. In the back, deep, deep recesses of our mind, we kind of knew something bad could happen.[22]

While Palihapitiya was mainly speaking about the corrosion of society as a whole, consider also what consequences those "short-term, dopamine-driven feedback loops" might have on an individual's mental health and well-being.

Here's the point: When looking at the dangers of social media, we must not only take into account our natural, biological reward responses, but also the fact that this new digital environment is hazardous *by design*.

"They Ghosted Me!"

I met nineteen-year-old Peter not long after he had attempted suicide—and had come very close to succeeding. In desperation, his father brought him to The Center on the day after Thanksgiving, seeking our help in his years-long battle with severe depression.

Peter shuffled into the room with his smartphone in hand and earbuds in place. His gaze flicked restlessly around the room, never making eye contact with me, our staff members, or his father. When I introduced myself, he said, "Happy Black Friday, Doc."

All through the intake process, Peter continued to periodically interact with his phone. He'd send a text or check on the status of a social media post and then quickly stash the phone in his hoodie pocket. For a moment, he would seem to focus on what was happening in the room, then, prompted by the device's silent buzz, he'd once again pull out the phone and drop his attention to his lap to respond.

If Peter had known what was coming next, I'm certain he'd have bolted for the door and never returned.

When people check in to The Center for residential treatment, the process always begins with a period of "detox" that includes being separated from all digital devices for at least seventy-two hours. We do this for practical reasons. We want clients to focus on the issues that brought them to our center, and not checking websites and texting with friends. What's more, this practice has real therapeutic value. Over the years, I've been increasingly astonished at what happens when people are deprived of their devices and disconnected from their online lives. Patients who are not otherwise addicted to a typical substance show many of the same telltale signs of physical withdrawal.

PATIENTS WHO ARE NOT OTHERWISE ADDICTED TO A TYPICAL SUBSTANCE SHOW MANY OF THE SAME TELLTALE SIGNS OF PHYSICAL WITHDRAWAL.

Peter's reaction was more severe than most. On day one, he became extremely agitated, perspiring and fidgeting constantly. His hands shook, and he complained of aches all over his body. In desperation, he begged for his phone back.

"I'm losing my streaks!" he finally cried, in real alarm.

Only after a little online research myself did I learn what that meant. He was referring to a common practice among teens using the social media site Snapchat. A streak begins when two "friends" send snaps back and forth for at least two consecutive days. The idea is to keep them going as long as possible—days, weeks, even months. Everyone you connect with can see how many streaks you have and how long they've lasted.

One fifteen-year-old boy described it this way in a *Business Insider* article on the phenomenon:

> A big part of it is social acceptance. … Having more streaks makes you feel more popular. … It's like a score. If you see your friends have a lot of streaks, you're like, "Whoa, that guy knows a lot of people." It shows their social status.[23]

It turns out Peter's distress went above and beyond the usual withdrawal we see in others because, to teens, streaks are more than a status symbol—they're a sign of commitment to a friendship. To break one is no small matter. Peter had invested huge amounts of time every day maintaining dozens of streaks. Some of those had lasted more than five hundred days. Because of this, he felt that losing his phone was a life-threatening event.

And yet, the truth was, Peter's immersion in the culture of streaks and his habit of deriving practically all his sense of self-worth and identity from social media was *literally* a danger to his life. Peter tried to kill himself because, on that day, several of his "friends" broke their long-lasting streaks in retaliation for a snap he'd sent that they didn't like.

"They ghosted me," he told me. "So I figured I'd be a real ghost and haunt [them]."

Eventually our whole-person treatment program helped Peter see the depth of his dependence on this kind of social media reward system and what it had cost him in terms of his health and well-being. He learned to regulate the amount of time he spent online and to decide for himself whether the "rewards" were worthwhile or not.

Social Self-Medication

Seeking out positive reinforcement isn't the only mood-altering function that engagement with social media can play. Its effect is not just to provide rewards, but also to deflect negative thoughts and emotions, or help us manipulate common challenges to our apparent advantage. Here are several ways social media can do just that.

1. SOCIAL MEDIA LETS US PRODUCE THE IDENTITY WE PRESENT TO THE WORLD.

Self-presentation in social settings is always a selective process. The identity we project with our peers is rarely the same face we show our family or bosses. Perhaps a better way to describe this natural process is to say we play different roles in different situations, depending on our place in the social framework and the goals we hope to achieve.

But social media has introduced an entirely new dimension to this. In essence, technology has turned everyone into a magazine publisher and video producer, putting all the same tools of spin and image manipulation at our fingertips. When we present ourselves now, it's to the entire, anonymous world.

> ALL THAT MAY FEEL GOOD FOR A TIME, BUT IT ISN'T SUSTAINABLE, BECAUSE IT LACKS A KEY INGREDIENT IN HEALTHY IDENTITY FORMATION: AUTHENTICITY.

This is especially enticing to young people, who already struggle to define their identities as a natural part of adolescence. Personal profiles exist right alongside those of famous celebrities and online influencers. These then become the template by which social media users shape their own appearance and persona. With the right photo enhancement filters or clever video editing techniques, teens can create their very own polished portfolio.

All that may feel good for a time, but it isn't sustainable, because it lacks a key ingredient in healthy identity formation: *authenticity*. This, in turn, only makes real relationships that much harder to establish and maintain, because it's not so easy to keep up polished appearances in person.

At the other end of the spectrum, social media gives a ready canvas for those who wish to present their lives as *harder* than they really are. Their status feeds are full of woeful pictures of visits to the emergency room or rants about every unfair thing that happens to them.

In ordinary face-to-face interactions, people who adopt these kinds of behaviors—one way or another—are likely to receive subtle (and not-so-subtle) signals of disapproval from others. From an early age, normal socialization is supposed to train us to avoid obvious pretense and drawing too much attention to ourselves. A report published by Penn State University describes how technology has disrupted that:

> With the emergence of social media, this process has moved into the virtual sphere. As a result, the individual may be tempted to construct a false self-presentation in order to be liked more by their peers. This self might be built on the false constructs that are offered by the media world: concepts of what is appealing, pretty, good, and tempting. All aspects of one's true self which do not conform with these notions may be put aside and rejected by the individual.[24]

In the worst-case scenario, this dynamic leaves young people stuck in early stages of identity formation, never moving on into self-actualization and maturity.

2. SOCIAL MEDIA BECOMES AN ESCAPE HATCH FOR OUR PROBLEMS.

Life isn't easy. No one can claim to be without their share of problems. As we've seen, excessive social media use can contribute to that list of challenging life circumstances by creating a variety of negative consequences itself.

THE INTERNET CAN BE ONE ENORMOUS ESCAPE HATCH.

In any case, checking up on the latest activity online can be great way to "check out" and avoid dealing with other things going on in your life. If facing some problem or struggling with procrastination makes you feel anxious, guilty, or overwhelmed, reaching for the phone or flipping open the laptop is an easy way to make those feelings go away … for a while. One recent study that focused on the users of Instagram concluded:

> As well as real-life problems, individuals sometimes feel the need to escape from their reality because of a lack of things to do and this can act as either as an escape from real-life troubles or to avoid thinking about unpleasant thoughts. … [A] small minority of individuals that successfully escape from reality by using Instagram may develop PIU [Problematic

Instagram Use] because it helps modify their mood, one of the dimensions for problematic use if combined with other negative components such as conflict.[25]

The Internet can be one enormous escape hatch. When life becomes too hard and stressful, when relationships become too unfulfilling or unsatisfactory, it's compelling to jump down into the rabbit hole of the Internet into a world of virtual reality. Do you understand it isn't totally real? Yes. But compared to how bad real life feels at the moment, you'll take virtual life anyway. Considering the amount of personal control you have over this virtual world compared to the lack of control felt in the real world, it's tempting to consider virtual an acceptable trade-off.

FIVE QUESTIONS TO ASK YOURSELF

If the Internet has become your personal escape hatch from life as you know it, I'd encourage you to think about why that is.

1. When you use the hatch, what are you escaping from?

2. How effective is it, if you have to keep using it again and again?

3. When you use it, where do you end up?

4. Are you more interested in running away from something than you are in arriving somewhere else?

5. Is your use of social media diverting your time and attention from the real issues of your life?

3. SOCIAL MEDIA GIVES THE ILLUSION OF INCREASED PRODUCTIVITY.

One of the positive effects of technology use often touted by its proponents is that it enables greater multitasking. The underlying assumption is that a person who can do five things at once—listen to a podcast, keep up a stream of texts and posts on Facebook, check incoming email, track pop-up news alerts, *and* work on a homework assignment—is five times more efficient and productive than others.

> WE MAY FEEL LIKE OUR ENGINES ARE FIRING ON ALL CYLINDERS, BUT IN FACT WE'RE SPUTTERING AND MISFIRING WITHOUT EVEN REALIZING IT.

The actual math is not so clear-cut. Research has shown that, while using digital technology increases the *quantity* of things you can do at once, it dramatically reduces the *quality* of the result. In other words, effective multitasking—a sort of super power claimed by some people to justify paying constant attention to their devices—is a myth. We may *feel* like our engines are firing on all cylinders, but in fact we're sputtering and misfiring without even realizing it.

Science can now back up that statement with evidence. Functional Magnetic Resonance Imaging is a technique for measuring what is happening in the brain in real time. The technology has been used to map neural activity when someone is doing more than one thing at once. The results offer proof of a common-sense belief: So long as two actions use different parts of the brain— say reading and listening to instrumental music—no conflict exists. But when two tasks both require the attention of the *same* area of the brain—reading and listening to music with lyrics—the trouble starts. Focus flickers back and forth between the two, degrading the efficiency of both.

This condition even has a name: *continuous partial attention*. That phrase was coined by a former Apple and Microsoft executive Linda Stone: "Continuous partial attention is an always-on, anywhere, anytime, anyplace behavior that involves an artificial sense of constant crisis."[26] That's because it is motivated by a desire to not miss anything and to be a live node on the network—to be connected.[27]

This description reminds me the frenetic energy of a pinball machine. In a state of continuous partial attention, we are like the little metal ball, careening and colliding off of every new stimulus we come into contact with, unable to rest, reflect, or even complete something before moving on. By definition, to be in a state of partial *attention* also means to be constantly, partially *distracted*.

In that condition, it's no surprise that important tasks are done only partially well—or even not at all.

As we've already seen, the role social media plays in continuous partial attention goes far beyond simply being one of many distractions. Because of the way it plays on our neurological reward system, social networking becomes a hyperactive pinball machine keeping the ball bouncing far more energetically—and for far longer—than it otherwise might.

I hope you'll agree by now that, whether or not social media use meets the technical criteria defining an addictive behavior, it certainly can trigger mood-altering effects in some people that are similar to other addictions—and just as dangerous to mental health and well-being. In the next section, I'll show you why that's true.

CHAPTER 3

The Depression Trap

How Social Media Contributes to Depression

Widespread social media use is still just a few decades old. The actual effects of too much screen time are still coming into focus, based on more and more scientific study. But, as I said previously, ample research has emerged in recent years to demonstrate that social media use contributes significantly to depression in a variety of ways.

Numerous studies point to adverse mental health effects in young people when they spend too much time engaged in online activity. A University of Pittsburgh School of Medicine study, for instance, concluded that exposure to "highly idealized representations of peers on social media elicits feelings of envy and the distorted belief that others lead happier, more successful lives"—which can actually cause depression, the authors wrote.[28]

I read with interest an article by Tufts School of Medicine professor Nassir Ghaemi, MD, titled "Snapchat Depression." Dr. Ghaemi writes:

> Even five years ago, I believed that most depression in teenagers was a sign of psychiatric disease. I don't believe that any longer. ... Instead, I've come to conclude that most of it is caused by increased engagement with smartphones, digital technology, and social media. Together, they are triggering what the nonprofit Culture Reframed calls a new "public health crisis of the digital age." ... The more depressed adolescents are, the more they use social media; the more they use social media, the more depressed they are. It's a vicious cycle.[29]

I can confirm from firsthand experience—after working with hundreds of clients over several decades—that the misuse of technology has a direct impact on the severity of depressive symptoms. It's why I have made addressing this behavior a key part of the whole-person approach to healing with all of the clients who come to The Center: A Place of Hope and in much of my speaking and writing.

If we look to research for a link between social media and depression, we find it easily enough. The key lies in the word *misuse* and in how we define it. In other words, we're back where we started at the beginning of this book, acknowledging that technology itself is neither harmful nor beneficial. It's our own choices about how we use technology that will determine personal experience.

It's not important to decide right now which comes first—digital obsession or emotional depression. What matters is this: If you are already struggling with symptoms of depression, overusing social media— or using it in unhealthy ways— can make matters much worse.

IF YOU ARE ALREADY STRUGGLING WITH SYMPTOMS OF DEPRESSION, OVERUSING SOCIAL MEDIA CAN MAKE MATTERS MUCH WORSE.

Isolation

A common feature of practically every Internet activity is that it's solitary. Sure, you may be messaging or chatting or gaming with others online, but generally, you are physically alone. This isolation can be damaging in many ways, but two in particular have negative consequences for people suffering from depression or wanting to avoid it.

First, interacting with others only through electronic media filters our communication and strips away a huge range of important nonverbal signals. Researchers estimate that anywhere from 65 to 85 percent of all communication takes place through nonverbal cues, such as eye contact, facial expression, hand gestures, posture, and so on. While we can choose our words carefully—and even use language to say things that are utterly untrue—it's nearly impossible to manipulate our subconscious signals. In other words, most of us tell the truth with body language. If you want to know what a person really thinks and who they really are, you have to be in personal contact with them.

REAL CONNECTION BY ELECTRONIC MEANS IS IMPOSSIBLE.

The Internet may provide the appearance of intimacy, but it's an illusion. Real connection by electronic means is impossible. Essentially, online relationships skip normal development and often create a sense of "instant intimacy," which is not true emotional closeness.

This has negative implications for someone who conducts most or all of their relationships online and is also struggling with depression. That person already feels damaged and deficient, probably convinced that's how everyone else sees them as well. Terse social media comments alone can easily be interpreted in a way that reinforces this belief, whereas face-to-face contact might include an abundance of nonverbal clues to the contrary. Furthermore, isolation hides the nonverbal cues you would otherwise send, letting people who care about you know that you're in distress and need help.

IF YOU WANT TO KNOW WHAT A PERSON REALLY THINKS AND WHO THEY REALLY ARE, YOU HAVE TO BE IN PERSONAL CONTACT WITH THEM.

Second, isolation enables us to create "false personas"—virtual identities we present in cyberspace that bear little resemblance to who we actually are. These alter egos allow us to adopt traits we ordinarily shun in face-to-face relationships: verbal aggression and overly explicit sexual communications, for example. Or they enable us to hide away all evidence of distress and creeping dysfunction in our real lives.

What a person seeking to heal from depression needs most of all is to focus attention on his or her life as it really is, to take stock of unhelpful conditions in the real world, and to accept support from real people.

False Intimacy *with* So Many "Friends"

This leads us to a related issue that can contribute to depression: the problem of having dozens, hundreds, or thousands of online friends but not feeling particularly close to many (or any) of them. Now, it might be that social media allows you to stay connected and up to date with real-life friends in ways that might be difficult or impossible to otherwise. For instance, if a long-time friend of yours lives far away, social media can keep you informed about day-to-day activities. That's a positive use of Facebook and other platforms.

But the problem that arises (and it arises frequently these days) is when your so-called connections to online friends leave you feeling disconnected to living, breathing people. In real life, what matters most is the quality of relationships, not the quantity of friends or followers.

> IN REAL LIFE, WHAT MATTERS MOST IS THE QUALITY OF RELATIONSHIPS, NOT THE QUANTITY OF FRIENDS OR FOLLOWERS.

Before the rise of online technology, frequent social contact made it harder to hide from each other. Now it's possible to have virtual communities where you never actually see or hear another person. With relationships occurring only through screens, if happening at all, interactions are cursory and often superficial. Individuals have to take each other at face value—without ever seeing your face beyond the images carefully posted. Now you can hide in plain sight, spending a great deal of time and energy pretending you have hundreds of friends. You can "know" a lot of people without truly knowing them or feeling known by them.

YOU CAN "KNOW" A LOT OF PEOPLE WITHOUT TRULY KNOWING THEM OR FEELING KNOWN BY THEM.

When you reflect on your hundreds or thousands of friends on Facebook, how many would you call at 3:00 in the morning with a crisis? If you suddenly became unemployed, thrown into financial insecurity, how many of those friends would call you or stop by in person to check on you? If a loved one passed away, how many of those people would offer you a shoulder to cry on?

Carefully evaluate this: As you struggle to keep up with your hundreds and sometimes thousands of "friends" on Facebook and other sites, are you sacrificing time that could otherwise be invested in real friendship? Is it possible that the larger your network, the more shallow your connections become? By immersing yourself in social media, are you choosing the quantity of friends over the quality?

Having lots of friends and dozens of "likes" on your Facebook status can be a boost to your confidence and sense of worth. But when things get tough, status likes and virtual comments won't replace a real shoulder to lean on or a real person to cry with. Psychologist Paula Durlofsky offers this balanced perspective:

> If we are using [social media] sites to build friendships, it's important to be aware of their limitations in order to avoid disappointment. When we find ourselves feeling left out, inadequate, irritable, or jealous after reading stories or viewing photos of our friends' activities, we can assume our cyber-relationships are not meeting our emotional needs.... It is also important to assess the quality of our nonvirtual relationships. This can be done by taking a hard look at the amount of time we spend with the people who are important to us. It is difficult, if not impossible, to replace the feelings of connection that manifest from having personal, genuine relationships.[30]

We all need close, committed relationships to maintain positive mental health—and to fend off depression. So let's spend ample time and energy investing in our real-life relationships, while recognizing that online friendships have inherent limitations.

Cyberbullying *and* Virtual Conflict

Over the past decade, we've been hearing more and more reports about cyberbullying and its damaging effects. With the use of various digital technologies, cyberbullying can take place on social media, messaging

PEOPLE CAN HIDE BEHIND THE GUISE OF ANONYMITY TO ELECTRONICALLY ABUSE THEIR VICTIMS.

platforms, gaming platforms, and mobile phones. It is repeated behavior aimed at scaring, angering, or shaming those who are targeted.

Although bullying has occurred for eons at playgrounds, street corners, and workplaces, digital technology has increased and expanded the ways harassment can be meted out. Cyberbullying is different from traditional bullying because people can hide behind the guise of anonymity to electronically abuse their victims. Screens provide a *smokescreen* from identification and responsibility. A person needs only a valid email address to create or participate in groups only, making it easy to set up fake accounts and bully anonymously. Remove the filters and feedbacks that govern in-person communication, and you take away the standards of conduct they are meant to regulate as well.

Sadly, this practice has become alarmingly widespread:

- ■ Over half of adolescents and teens have been bullied online, and about the same number have engaged in cyberbullying.

- More than 1 in 3 young people have experienced cyberthreats online.

- Over 25 percent of adolescents and teens have been bullied repeatedly through their cell phones or the Internet.

- Well over half of young people do not tell their parents when cyberbullying occurs.[31]

While normally thought of as a problem only among teens, cyberbullying can happen to anyone. According to the Pew Research Center, 41 percent of US adults report they've been the target of online harassment, including 18 percent who say the incidents were "severe," such as sustained stalking and threats of violence.[32]

It's no wonder that Stanford University psychiatrist Elias Aboujaoude, MD, calls this a serious public health problem:

> Although cyberbullying would not exist without Internet-related technologies, it is not just that more people are connected to the Internet that is causing it to spread; it is also how they are connected. The dizzying growth of social media and the intimate access they give to all sorts of loosely defined "friends" make them a bully's heaven and contribute to making cyberbullying a serious public health problem.... Cyberbullying is frequently associated with psychological distress. Cybervictims tend to have increased rates of depression, anxiety, insomnia, whereas cyberbullies are more likely to have problems with outward aggression, hyperactivity and substance use. A major concern is the increased risk of suicide, considered stronger than in traditional bullying.[33]

Here's the bottom line: The last thing a person suffering from depression—or at risk of becoming depressed—needs is exposure to a stream of merciless judgments and condemnations masquerading as a "chat" or a "comment." An unhealthy self-image is already a tripwire in their lives. Far from diffusing the danger, too much time on the Internet is an invitation to make matters worse.

FIVE TYPES OF CYBERBULLYING

Just as traditional bullying exists in a variety of forms, such as verbal abuse and physical violence, there are many different types of cyberbullying. According to experts at the organization End to Cyberbullying, there are five common forms.[34]

1. Harassment

Harassment involves the bully's offensive and malicious messages sent to an individual or a group, often repeated multiple times. *Cyberstalking* is a form of harassment that involves continual threatening and rude messages, sometimes leading to physical confrontation in the real world.

2. Flaming

Flaming refers to an online fight exchanged via emails, instant messaging, or chat rooms. It is a type of public bullying that often directs harsh language or images to a specific person.

3. Exclusion

Exclusion is the act of intentionally leaving an individual out from online groups such as chats and sites. Group members subsequently leave malicious comments and harass the person they singled out.

4. Outing

Outing is when a bully shares personal and private information, pictures, or videos about someone publicly. A person is "outed" when his information has been disseminated throughout the Internet.

5. Masquerading

Masquerading occurs when a bully creates a fake identity to harass someone anonymously. In addition, the bully might impersonate someone else to send malicious messages to the victim.

A Crisis *of* Comparison

It's long been recognized that "keeping up with the Joneses" is a big part of what keeps us all running the "rat race." Those may be outdated phrases these days, but the condition of unhealthy envy is still alive and well. It's admittedly difficult to avoid comparing the outward appearances of your neighbor's life to your own—jobs, cars, homes, overachieving kids, and exotic vacations—and concluding they must be better off and happier than you.

> "THE REASON WE STRUGGLE WITH INSECURITY IS BECAUSE WE COMPARE OUR BEHIND-THE-SCENES WITH EVERYONE ELSE'S HIGHLIGHT REEL."
>
> –Pastor Steven Furtick

Before the Internet, those we compared ourselves to were mostly flesh-and-blood people. They lived down the street or worked down the hall. It was at least possible to see them at their worst as well as their best. And they numbered in the dozens at the very most.

Now we compare ourselves to thousands, if not millions, of virtual "neighbors." And we see only what they allow us to see—photos of their pets, happy dinners with friends, far-flung excursions, kids getting academic awards, crossing the finish line at the Boston Marathon.

Most of this is posted by people who are friends in name only. It's a giant understatement to say that all this adds up to a managed and distorted view of who people really are and how they actually live. And that's before we account for perceptions created by advertisers that can be grossly manipulative, misleading, or outright false.

A person at risk for depression is already poised to believe that his or her life doesn't measure up to the lives of others. The Internet provides persuasive evidence they're right about that. As Pastor Steven Furtick said, "The reason we struggle with insecurity is because we compare our behind-the-scenes with everyone else's highlight reel."

When I was in graduate school, I learned about social psychologist Leon Festinger, who, in the mid-1950s, popularized "social comparison theory." This theory claims that people have a natural desire to assess our progress and status by comparing ourselves to others. When we make "upward" comparisons, we measure ourselves against people we feel inferior to. Given the "highlight reel" nature of social media, it is almost impossible to avoid upward comparisons, often causing us to experience dissatisfaction, desperation, and even depression.

I appreciate the perspective of science writer Rebecca Webber:

> Social media is like kerosene poured on the flame of social comparison, dramatically increasing the information about people that we're exposed to and forcing our minds to assess. In the past, we absorbed others' triumphs sporadically—the alumni bulletin would report a former classmate having made partner at the law firm or a neighbor would mention that his kid got into Harvard. Now such news is at our fingertips constantly, updating us about a greater range of people than we previously tracked, and we invite its sepia-filtered jolts of information into our commutes, our moments waiting in line for coffee, even our beds at 2 A.M.[35]

With social media, people are able to focus on key aspects of their lives, highlighting the positive and omitting anything they want to hide. While we are intimately aware of the daily trials and struggles of our own lives, our friends' lives appear to be a string of successes punctuated infrequently by minor setbacks that are handled with grace and poise. In an environment like this, it is easy to slip into comparing ourselves with others.

Toxic Content

While much of what you see on the Internet presents an overly rosy view of reality, other sites peddle the opposite extreme: nonstop doom and gloom. It's an alarming parade of war, famine, political strife, social injustice, and environmental catastrophe. It's almost as if news organizations, bloggers, filmmakers, chat group members, and millions of commenters have conspired to turn whole regions of cyberspace into a scene from Dante Alighieri's epic poem *Inferno*—where the entrance to hell was inscribed, "Abandon hope all ye who enter here!" Spend much time there, and you'll be convinced the world teeters on the edge of calamity and collapse every second of every day.

TURNING OFF THE SPIGOT AND CLEANING UP THE DIGITAL SLUDGE IS AN ESSENTIAL STEP TOWARD RECOVERY.

It isn't just the hyper-focus on bad news and disaster that brings us down, it's also the barrage of rumors, gossip, celebrity failures, sports scandals, and petty disputes that leave us discouraged and distressed. Writing in *Forbes* magazine, journalist Kalev Leetaru said, "Social media's rising tide has lifted all boats, elevating even the most horrific and toxic voices singularly fixated on tearing society apart and placing them equal with those informed and measured voices trying to bring us together."[36]

Sometimes the seemingly harmless social media features can be most grievous. The website TechTimes.com has an article that rated web users' most despised features:

> Internet users have decided that the "Like" button on sites like Facebook and Instagram is one of the most toxic features on social media. ... The poll revealed that triggering content, or content that reminds a person of negative or traumatic experience, is the element of social media that people think is the most toxic. This is followed by the "Like" button found in many of these online platforms, including Facebook that boasts of 1.59 billion daily active users (as of June 2019) and Instagram that has 500 million daily active users.[37]

It should come as no surprise that a steady diet of "digital distortion" and persistent pessimism endangers mental health and magnifies depression symptoms. It rarely leads to healthy or effective political engagement on important issues. In fact, exposure to "doom porn," as it is often called, simply reinforces feelings of powerlessness and despair. That's why, to a person struggling to overcome depression, it's positively toxic.

Turning off the spigot and cleaning up the digital sludge is an essential step toward recovery.

A Sense *of* Wasting Time

It's no surprise that we are wired to enjoy being creative and productive. We are, after all, made in the image of our Creator—and God is the epitome of creativity and productivity! (Look at what Genesis tells us he accomplished in seven days!)

We are also wired to need intimacy and connection with our own thoughts and emotions, with other people, and with God. In addition, our bodies, minds, and emotions thrive when we get sleep, exercise, and spend time outdoors.

These are some of the key elements that make up a healthy, balanced, satisfying life. When we incorporate these things into our days, we are more likely to fall asleep at night feeling satisfied and fulfilled.

Social media, to be honest, is often a huge time-vacuum that accomplishes none of those things. When our time on social media goes unchecked, we can spend hours of our day and have nothing to show for it—besides the vague emptiness and insecurities that social media can foster.

And when we lose hours to random browsing and surfing, feeling unfilled is just the beginning. We can also begin to feel overwhelmed because our lack of productivity is catching up to us and creating stress from life and work tasks that are going undone.

In other words, the fallout from slipping into the black hole of wasted hours online can wreak havoc with our lives and our emotions.

WE ARE WIRED TO NEED INTIMACY AND CONNECTION WITH OUR OWN THOUGHTS AND EMOTIONS, WITH OTHER PEOPLE, AND WITH GOD.

Here's another aspect to consider: A hallmark symptom of serious depression is an inability to keep up with daily responsibilities and obligations. Depressed people feel drained of the energy and motivation needed to complete even the most commonplace tasks. Lots of factors converge to make this so, including poor nutrition, lack of exercise, unhelpful sleep habits, and volatile emotions. An often-overlooked item that also belongs on the list is *time leakage*.

A person who is depressed will spend hours searching for distractions and ways to fill time. The Internet presents an infinite warehouse full of options. One click leads to a hundred more possibilities. Social media is a bottomless pit of posts, likes, follows, and comments—and before you know it, whole evenings or whole days have disappeared. When that happens, you might fall deeper down the rabbit hole of hopelessness and despair. Reclaiming your time and how you spend it is a vital step in reclaiming your life from depression.

Emotional Contagion

Did you know that emotions can be contagious? Science agrees and, in fact, researchers have been studying "emotional contagion" for years. This is the phenomenon where the emotions of one person in a group—a family, a work staff, even a collection of friends showing up in a social media feed—can spread to others in the same group. In essence, people involuntarily absorb and adopt emotions transmitted through online communication.

Emotional contagion has both downsides and upsides. Positive expressions of emotion—smiles, joy, optimism—are catching. In fact, researchers Nicholas Christakis and James Fowler have concluded that for every happy friend you have, you increase your own probability of being happy by nearly 10 percent.[38] Likewise, negative emotions are transmissible too.

Even negative body language—like frowns and crossed arms—can spread like wildfire in a group. And studies show that "secondhand depression" does indeed occur, meaning that people who have depressed spouses are more likely to struggle with depression themselves.

> RESEARCH HAS SHOWN THAT HAPPINESS, ANGER, SADNESS, AND EVERYTHING IN BETWEEN CAN BE PASSED ON TO AN INDIVIDUAL THROUGH SOCIAL MEDIA.

It's not a new idea. We've all heard folk wisdom like, "Birds of a feather flock together," or "If you want to see your future, look at your friends." We are just now gaining a better understanding how emotions spread among groups of people. So what does this mean for you and your social media experiences?

Research has shown that happiness, anger, sadness, and everything in between can be passed on to an individual through social media. One study examined 3,800 randomly selected social media users, testing the contagiousness of the emotional tones of the content they viewed online. The study found that emotional states are easily manipulated through social media, and simply reading emotionally charged posts can transfer emotional states to the reader.[39] Your exposure to negative rants, tragic news, pathos, drama, and conflict in your virtual friend circles are not without impact. And yet, because emotional contagion typically works on a subconscious level, you can find yourself mirroring the negativity to which you are exposed on social media, without ever realizing that's what you're doing.

Understanding the connection between negative expressions you see online and your real-life struggles is the first step to unplugging and protecting your mood and your emotions.

Physical Stagnation

We've already mentioned that most technology use is solitary. Now let's consider the fact that it's also *stationary*. Simple observation will confirm this. A person playing video games will remain in virtually the same position for hours. Someone surfing online will sit hunched over a keyboard, sometimes barely looking up for long periods of time.

Health risks associated with such a sedentary lifestyle are well documented: high blood pressure, heart disease, type-2 diabetes, certain types of cancer, obesity, reduced immune system function, and *depression and anxiety*. One study titled, "The Benefits of Exercise for the Clinically Depressed," noted that "depressed patients are less fit and have diminished physical work capacity on the order of 80 percent to 90 percent of age-predicted norms, which in turn may contribute to other physical health problems."[40]

For people struggling with depression, even moderate exercise is a key component in regulating emotions and activating the body's chemistry that lifts a person's mood. The *British Journal of Sports Medicine* reported that walking thirty minutes each day alleviated symptoms of depression more quickly than many pharmaceutical antidepressants.[41] What's more, a Duke University study found that those who exercised regularly were four times more likely to remain depression-free six months after the start of treatment than those who took medication.[42]

Putting two and two together, it's easy to see how overuse of technology—inevitably stationary and physically stagnant—will stand in the way of lasting healing from depression. This relates directly to social media use, since many people spend hours and hours scrolling through posts and newsfeeds when they could be enjoying the benefits of physical activity. Now would be a good time to evaluate if your online time is crowding out your exercise time, and make adjustments accordingly.

Seeking Validation *from* Unreliable Sources

As humans, we are wired to seek approval and validation—and there's nothing wrong with that. Healthy individuals meet their need for validation through a variety of means. The problem arises, however, when we are overly focused on gaining that approval and validation from a single source: other people.

There are actually several ways to get this need met, with validation from others being just one. Another is called *self-validation* and it involves the process of allowing yourself to acknowledge your efforts and feelings in a way that makes it unnecessary to seek those things from others. And if you are a person of faith, you can get this need met from your relationship with God and what the Bible says about your worth to him.

Again, wanting feedback and approval from others is hardly a new thing. Remember the Bible story of Eve eating fruit that had been forbidden, then sharing some with her husband, Adam? Was she seeking his approval? Did she need his agreement that her decision had been the right one? If social media had existed back then, would Eve have posted a photo of an apple along with the comment, "Look what I'm having for dinner!" and then checked every few minutes to see how many "likes" and "shares" she had garnered?

SOCIAL MEDIA HAS MADE IT POSSIBLE TO GARNER IMMEDIATE ATTENTION FOR ANY ACTION OR THOUGHT YOU CAN PUBLICIZE IN A POST, TWEET, COMMENT, PHOTO, OR VIDEO.

While our need for feedback and approval isn't new, social media has certainly put a whole new spin on the experience. Social media has made it possible to garner immediate attention for any action or thought you can publicize in a post, tweet, comment, photo, or video.

In fact, the phenomenon has led to people going to extreme (and dangerous) lengths to gain attention—like the young woman who achieved her goal of viral fame by posting a video of herself licking an airplane toilet seat during the coronavirus pandemic. She achieved her goal, but at what cost? Health? Dignity? And how did she feel when her fame drew fire from people who, rather than approving her behavior, indicated their disgust and shock? Did she feel rejected? Remorseful? Embarrassed? Depressed?

> PLACING YOUR SELF-ESTEEM IN THE HANDS OF VIRTUAL FRIENDS SEEKING DISTRACTION OR ENTERTAINMENT OVER TRUE CONNECTION IS A VULNERABLE PLACE TO BE.

You might think that's an extreme example, and it is. You may say that you would never be that desperate for social media validation, and you are probably right. But the truth is that social media drives us to care more than we should about drawing the attention, likes, shares, comments, follows, and retweets of people in a virtual social circle. And what's alarming is that many of the people we add to our virtual social circle are folks we barely know, don't spend time with, and maybe don't even like in real life!

Social media leaves us asking questions we simply didn't need to ask twenty years ago: What does it say about me if no one likes my post? Why did that person unfriend me? Why don't I have more followers?

In a twist to the philosophical question, "If a tree falls in the woods and no one hears it, did it make a sound?" we find ourselves wondering, "If it doesn't end up drawing approval on social media, how important could it have possibly been?"

The point is, when you seek validation for who you are and what you do from unreliable sources—such as social media sites—it can leave you feeling deflated, disheartened, and possibly depressed. Placing your self-esteem in the hands of virtual friends seeking distraction or entertainment over true connection is a vulnerable place to be. Protect yourself by replacing validation on social media with validation from real life relationships with people who know and care about you, validation from yourself, and validation from God.

ELEVEN SYMPTOMS OF DEPRESSION

A recent report by the National Institute of Mental Health revealed that 16.2 million adults and 3.1 million teenagers between age twelve and seventeen had endured a recent "major depressive episode." Around two-thirds of those people suffered life impairments that were rated as "severe."[43]

Because depression is often overlooked and misunderstood, it's important to recognize its symptoms. These include:

1. Persistent sad, anxious, or "empty" mood

2. Feelings of hopelessness and pessimism

3. Feelings of guilt, worthlessness, and helplessness

4. Loss of interest or pleasure in hobbies and activities

5. Decreased energy, fatigue, being "slowed down"

6. Difficulty concentrating, remembering, making decisions

7. Difficulty sleeping, early morning awakening, or oversleeping

8. Appetite and/or weight changes

9. Thoughts of death or suicide, suicide attempts

10. Restlessness, irritability

11. Persistent physical symptoms

SIGNS TO WATCH FOR

Everyone is different and there is no specific amount of time spent on social media, frequency with which you check for updates, or number of posts you make that indicates your use is becoming unhealthy. Rather, it has to do with the impact social media has on your mood and other aspects of your life, along with your motivations for using it.

The mental health website, HelpGuide, lists these indicators as signs to watch for.[44]

■ **You spend more time with your social media "friends" than with your real-life friends.**
Has social media become a substitute for offline interactions with living, breathing people? Even if you're out with friends, you still feel the need to constantly check social media, often driven by feelings that others may be having more fun than you.

■ **You compare yourself with others on social media and feel inferior.**
Drawing unfavorable comparisons can lead to low self-esteem or negative body image. It can hinder gratitude for the blessings you have and the God-given talents you possess.

■ **You feel distracted at school or work.**
Rather than staying focused on the tasks in front of you,
your strong inclination is to check your social media sites.
You might feel pressure to post regular content about
yourself and see the latest posts from others.

■ **You have little or no time for self-reflection.**
With your time taken up with social media, you have no
space left for introspection and spiritual pursuits. If you
set aside little time for journaling, inspirational reading,
or prayer, your use of social media is likely out of balance.

■ **You engage in risky behavior in order to gain "likes."**
You play dangerous pranks, post embarrassing material,
cyberbully others, or access your phone while driving or in
other unsafe situations.

■ **Your sleep patterns are disrupted.**
Do you check social media last thing at night, first thing
in the morning, or even when you wake up in the night?
The light from phones and other devices can disrupt your
sleep, which in turn can have a serious impact on your
mental health.

- **You feel worse, not better, after a social media session.**
Rather than helping to alleviate negative feelings and boost your mood, you feel more anxious, depressed, or lonely after using social media.

■ ■ ■

REAL CONNECTIONS HAPPEN IN REAL LIFE

Swiss novelist and playwright Max Frisch once said, "Technology is the knack of so arranging the world that we don't have to experience it."

Life cannot be arranged; it must be lived. Life needs to be accepted and lived out in truth. The grass may appear greener on the Internet, but it is virtual turf.

People post pictures and upload videos and create content that isn't complete and isn't fully accurate. Written thoughts and feelings are low-bandwidth and don't come with visual and audible context. You don't get to look them in the eye or see the tilt of the head. You don't get to hear the tone of voice, the snort, or the sigh. Even the most transparent of us have blind sides and unwitting evasiveness.

Real connection is best conducted in real life.

CHAPTER 4

Take Back Control

Strategies for Healthy Use of Social Media

Despite the inherent downsides and dangers related to social media, the fact remains that social media offers many benefits as well.

- For example, you may already have had the experience of using social media to stay in touch with faraway family members or reconnect with good friends from your past.

- Social media is also used by many businesses to connect with customers and potential new clients.

- Neighborhoods form private groups to share helpful information.

- And connecting with people who share niche interests has never been easier. Whether you love books, jogging, woodworking, or pet goats, you can connect with others in your own community (or around the world) who love the same thing.

- In addition, if you're looking for education, encouragement, and solutions for a challenge you're facing, you can undoubtedly find some resources on social media. Groups devoted to health issues, parenting challenges, healing from trauma, and much more use social media platforms for connection, education, and support.

So the benefits of social media are real.

The challenge, of course, lies in finding healthy, balanced ways to enjoy some of the benefits without damaging your esteem, mental health, and real-life relationships in the process. Even with an intentional, proactive approach to social media use, you're sure to encounter many dangers, which could lead to depression.

We've already talked about the addictive nature of social media. There are a number of contributing factors, including your own brain chemistry, 24/7 accessibility, and sophisticated algorithms that customize your newsfeed to make it as enticing as possible.

In other words, social media is an intoxicating blend of distraction and rewards that can make it hard to ignore—and easy to get sucked into despite very real perils to the quality of your productivity, emotions, sleep, relationships, and more.

All that to say, a healthy, balanced approach to social media is unlikely to occur on its own. Unchecked, social media can have a slow-growing negative impact, compromising the quality of your life in ways you never anticipated— nor would have agreed to had you known.

If you're not intentional about learning and applying strategies that can help you enjoy a beneficial and balanced relationship with social media, you'll be left at the mercy of the destructive elements of what is truly a doubled-edged force in our society.

Here are nine actions you can start taking today that will help you engage online in healthy ways—and avoid depression.

1. EVALUATE YOUR "WHY."

If you're spending a lot of time on social media, there are reasons why. You are looking for something—or getting something—out of the time you spend scrolling. Understanding the "why" can leave you better equipped to meet those same needs through healthier, and less addictive, means.

- Perhaps you are lonely, bored, or you are looking for reasons to procrastinate tackling less pleasant overdue tasks.

- Are you looking for the surge of dopamine and approval you feel when someone likes your photo or post?

- Is social media an easy replacement for face-to-face relationships that are more complex and require more of you than a few lines of text?

- Does social media allow you to present to the world an uncontested image of someone you're not—but wish you were?

- It's possible you're not even sure what you're seeking but have simply fallen into the deeply engrained habit of reaching for your phone dozens—even hundreds—of times every day.

What is your "why"?

Journal about it. Process the question with a spouse, friend, or counselor. Sometimes simple awareness evokes immediate change. Other times, awareness is the first step in a series of steps toward transformation.

Either way, awareness is powerful.

Limiting the negative influence of social media in your life doesn't mean giving up the benefits you are getting from using these platforms. It means finding more diverse and healthier ways of getting those needs met.

2. PAY ATTENTION TO YOUR EMOTIONS AND TO THE MESSAGES EVOKING THOSE EMOTIONS.

After you've spent time on social media, how do you feel?

- Energized or fatigued? Lifted or deflated? Hopeful or cynical? Connected or alone?

- Do you feel refreshed after an entertaining break, or dread at having to log off and face real life?

- Do you feel anxious? Jealous? Inferior? Depressed?

Your emotions tell you a lot about how you are being impacted by social media.

If social media is having a detrimental impact on your emotions, pay attention to the messages you are being exposed to while online. Are you being bombarded by critical feedback, anxiety-inducing news, or cyberbullying? Is your newsfeed filled with carefully curated images and posts of friends who would love for you to believe their lives are perfect?

We may think we are looking at everything with a discerning eye, but the truth is that what we expose ourselves to daily impacts the way we perceive the world and ourselves—and those perceptions influence the emotions we feel.

3. TAILOR YOUR SOCIAL MEDIA EXPERIENCE TO BE UPLIFTING.

The *bad* news is that social media algorithms tailor your experience based on what you've viewed in the past. That means that when you click on scary news articles, the posts of your most pessimistic friends, or sponsored content that leaves you feeling down, you're going to see even more of that kind of content in your newsfeed.

BE INTENTIONAL ABOUT WHAT YOU CLICK ON, CHOOSING UPLIFTING POSTS.

The *good* news is that social media algorithms tailor your experience based on what you've viewed in the past. That means you can begin today changing the stream of content to which you are exposed. Avoid the temptation to click on posts that ultimately leave you cynical, jealous, discouraged, or depressed. Instead, be intentional about what you click on, choosing uplifting posts. The same rule applies to what you choose to comment on and engage with.

Finally, the groups, companies, and individuals with which you connect also help determine what you see on social media.

So the strategy is simple: Stop clicking on content you know isn't good for you. Unfollow companies and groups posting content that makes you feel bad. And if you have friends who post things that are upsetting to you, consider unfollowing them (or staying connected but hiding their posts).

Instead, search out groups or friends posting content that leaves you encouraged. Engage with those folks. Ignore the rest. You'll appreciate the difference it makes in the content you receive.

4. LOOK FOR HEALTHY REPLACEMENTS, ONLINE OR OFFLINE.

There are lots of other things you can do online other than browse social media. Research an interesting topic or project. Take an online class. Get moving with workout videos on YouTube. Learn a new language. Listen to podcasts.

You can even use your online time to inspire yourself to do something offline. For example, do an online search for walking trails in your city, and then head outdoors. Or research recipes that represent your ethnic heritage, and then head to the store for ingredients. And as long as you're walking or cooking, why not invite friends to join you? Which leads us to the next strategy.

5. SCHEDULE TIME TO SPEND WITH YOUR REAL-LIFE FRIENDS.

I'll be the first to admit that virtual friendships take less investment and effort than face-to-face interactions. But real-life relationships provide the meaningful interactions that most help us feel connected, needed, and known.

Plus, online communication suffers without the help of nonverbal cues and deeper connection—and when it does, there's very little constructive working out of disagreements or offenses.

Dr. Jim Taylor, a specialist in the psychology of sport and parenting, addresses the dangers of "wired life," calling social media "social lite" and "social safe" because it limits the richness of human interactions as well as keeps relationships at a comfortable distance.[45]

So host dinners. Plan game nights. Get together for coffee. Hike a trail with a friend. And by all means, when you are together, agree to put down your phones!

6. PLAN AND LIMIT YOUR TIME ON SOCIAL MEDIA.

Social media is addictive enough that, without a plan, you can find yourself spending way more time—and reaping more negative side effects—than you thought possible.

Most smartphones allow you to monitor and limit the time you are spending on social media. If you use an iPhone, Google how to turn on "Screen Time," or "Digital Well-being" on an Android. There are even apps you can download to your phone that will lock your phone for a set period of time to help you unplug. These apps show you exactly how much time you've spent on social media. Sometimes seeing the number of hours can steel your resolve to spend your time more wisely.

SOMETIMES THE BEST WAY TO CUT BACK ON SOMETHING ISN'T FORCING LIMITS, BUT FILLING OUR TIME WITH HEALTHIER PLEASURES.

It's also good to be aware of *where* you are most likely to over-consume social media. For many people, smartphones provide the most consistent and tempting access. If that's the case, consider removing Facebook and other social media from your phone altogether. You may find that you spend less time browsing social media on your desktop computer than your phone. If so, that one choice to remove the temptation from your handheld device may bring your life into better balance.

Of course, sometimes the best way to cut back on something isn't forcing limits, but filling our time with healthier pleasures so there's simply less time to think about—much less practice—the habit we want to break. Adding exercise, social gatherings, a local class, volunteering, or a *real* hobby (browsing is not a hobby) to your day can lessen the temptation to turn to social media when you have an extra ten minutes (which always turns into thirty, right?).

You can also try limiting your exposure to social media to specific windows of time, like during your lunch break at work or only after the dinner dishes are done.

7. THINK OF SOCIAL MEDIA AS A SNACK, NOT A BUFFET.

Whether we follow a food guideline or not, most of us understand that the body needs healthy food, and that there will be repercussions if we consume a steady diet of snacks and desserts. Obesity, heart disease, brain fog, high blood pressure, and more can be the result of a wrong diet.

In a same way, we need to change our perspective about social media. When we think of social media as an occasional or daily "snack" or "dessert," it helps us visualize the kind of healthy balance we need to embrace. To avoid detrimental effects, social media is best served as a treat enjoyed in moderation, rather than the buffet line at which we graze all day long.

8. PLAN AND IMPLEMENT A SOCIAL MEDIA DETOX.

It's possible that you've tried many of these strategies and still have not been able to embrace a healthier, more balanced approach to social media. Or at least not consistently. Perhaps you've reduced your dependence on social media for short periods of time, only to have the hours creep back up again.

If this has been your experience, consider a "social media detox" for a week. To start, identify a friend who can serve as an accountability buddy, someone with whom you can check in and talk about struggles and victories along the way. Then delete social media apps from your handheld devices and if you know you'll be tempted to log in on your desktop, search for tips on blocking sites on your computer. This can often be accomplished in Tools/Internet Options. There are also programs and apps that will help you do the same thing.

> THE LESS OFTEN YOU REACH FOR YOUR PHONE IN A GIVEN DAY, THE LESS LIKELY YOU ARE TO FIND YOURSELF CHECKING YOUR SOCIAL MEDIA FEEDS.

To further reduce temptation, bring back some other helpful gadgets (like alarm clocks, calendars, and watches) that have been replaced by your phone. The less often you reach for your phone in a given day, the less likely you are to find yourself checking your social media feeds.

A social media detox doesn't need to be forever, but it does need to be long enough to help you develop some new habits.

9. SEE YOURSELF THROUGH THE EYES OF PEOPLE WHO KNOW YOU BEST.

Sometimes the thing that keeps us from setting intentional boundaries with social media is denial. Ask the people who know you best—your spouse, children, best friends—what they've observed about your relationship with social media. Ask them if they've ever wished you would put down the phone and pay more attention to them, and how that has made them feel. Even when we are unwilling to protect ourselves from being hurt by an addictive habit we've embraced, we may be willing to take stronger action when we see people we love being hurt by our choices.

Social media has the potential for great good. But too much of a good thing can be just as destructive as something we know from the get-go is bad for us. In fact, the legitimate benefits of social media can keep us in denial as we fall victim to its very legitimate dangers.

Take back control of your life by setting very intentional boundaries. Only then can you reap the benefits without losing your joy in the process.

SEVEN TIPS FOR A TECHNOLOGY DETOX

Many studies show how technology can contribute to high levels of stress, strain on relationships and family, attention deficit disorder symptoms, certain mental disorders, and even health problems, possibly including cancer. As much as it may pain you to consider, it could be time for a detox, a voluntary reduction in your use of technology. The more things you're hooked into, the harder this will be and the more anxiety it will produce. But if conducted in a thoughtful manner, a detox can help you release some of the negative buildup of your technology use and give you the break you need to make better choices going forward.

Here are some steps to help guide you through this process.

1. Plan Your Progress.

Technology is so much a part of our lives, you'll need to be intentional about what you're going to give up, for what reason, and for how long. This isn't something you can do haphazardly, or you'll just end up reverting back to old habits. The key word is *intentional*. You want to go into this with eyes wide open so you can monitor and respond to your reactions to digital deprivation. Develop a plan, then stick to it. This will help you weather the squalls of anxiety that can threaten to overturn your best intentions.

2. Start With a Small Break.

You may consider a tech detox as a sort of digital fast or cleanse, and cringe at the concept, thinking you're going to have to do the cyber equivalent of never having another piece of chocolate while living on tofu and grapefruit. Relax. Those kinds of diets don't work with food, and I doubt they'd work for technology either. Instead, start with baby steps.

For example, if you're going to go see a movie with your family or attend your child's soccer game, leave your cell phone in the car. Give yourself permission to spend a few hours concentrating on just one thing—enjoying the movie or game with your family. If you're the kind of person who needs to review email every fifteen minutes, give yourself permission to check it less frequently, say, every hour. Start small and allow yourself to experience incremental victories.

3. Don't Just Reduce or Remove. Replace, Too.

When you decide to stop doing something you enjoy, you create a void. Whatever you were doing filled some sort of need, and ceasing that activity will cause that need to resurface. If you don't fill that need with something else, it's going to feel like an enormous black hole. Instead, be proactive. As you decide what you're going to reduce, determine something positive, healthy, and uplifting you're going to replace it with.

Suppose you decide you're going to reduce your amount of Facebook time during the week, from daily to only every other day. On those non-Facebook days, you could arrange to meet in person with a friend and go for a walk or meet for coffee and an old-fashioned conversation. You could walk the dog or window shop with a family member. You could finally tackle clearing out that extra bedroom or painting the hall. If you're filling up the time with something good, doing without the digital won't seem so bad.

> REGAIN CONTROL OVER YOUR DEVICES, YOUR TIME, AND YOUR PSYCHE.

4. Clarify Your Goals.

Along those same lines, be specific about why you're doing the detox. Write down your goals, and then reduce them to short, memorable phrases you can repeat to yourself when the going gets tough and you're tempted to Google the latest gossip.

5. Set Clear Rules, and Stick to Them.

Decide beforehand what the parameters of your detox are going to be. If you decide not to check work emails from home in the evening, specify the hours you can check them. The more specific the parameters, the less room there will be for cheating. And then, don't cheat. Just because you made the rules doesn't mean you get to break them. This is also why it's important to start small. The fewer the rules, the easier it will be to keep them. Then, as you rack up victories, you can expand your goals. As you gain successes, the first targets will begin to seem natural and less restrictive.

Be sure to determine the consequences ahead of time as well. You don't want to cheat, but at some point you probably will. So when planning your detox, also plan for failure. Decide ahead of time how you're going to reset when you do take that call during the school play or smuggle your phone into your luggage during a weekend away. Nobody is perfect, and you won't keep your convictions perfectly, so give yourself a break. Know a side trip is coming, and provide yourself a way back to the straight and narrow.

6. Take Advantage of What You've Learned.

The goal should not be merely to see how long you can do something, knowing that you're just going to dive back in with renewed passion, enthusiasm, and a sigh of relief. One goal of a tech detox should be to learn that you can truly live without it, but that's not the only goal. You should also strive to use the detox to learn more about yourself and how you interact with technology in all aspects of your being—what I call the *whole person*: emotionally, relationally, physically, and spiritually. By paying attention to each of these areas during a detox, you can learn how technology is useful to you in each area, and how it can actually be harmful.

7. Take the Next Step.

Armed with the knowledge you've gained about yourself and your technology use, establish new long-term boundaries. Knowledge is not enough to modify behavior. You must apply what you've learned in order to change patterns. Learning is like growing; if you stop, you atrophy. Take what you've learned, keep growing, and keep moving toward a more positive and healthy integration of technology in your life. Technology is always changing, and you need to stay flexible in order to keep up without becoming controlled by it again.

Notes

1   Igor Pantic, "Online Social Networking and Mental Health," *Cyberpsychology, Behavior and Social Networking* 10 (October 2014): 652–657.

2   Shainna Ali, "Could You Be Addicted to Technology?" *Psychology Today* (February 12, 2018).

3   Neil Postman, *Amusing Ourselves to Death: Public Discourse in the Age of Show Business* (Penguin Books, 1985).

4   "You Tube for Press," YouTube: *https://www.youtube.com/about/press*.

5   Mansoor Iqbal, "Netflix Revenue and Usage Statistics (2020)," *Business of Apps* (June 23, 2020).

6   Andrew Perrin and Madhu Kumar, "About three-in-ten U.S. adults say they are 'almost constantly' online," Fact Tank, Pew Research Center (July 25, 2019).

7   "Public Health Implications of Excessive Use of the Internet, Computers, Smartphones and Similar Electronic Devices," World Health Organization (August 27–29, 2014).

8   Anthony Robinson, Aaron Bonnette, Krista Howard, Natalie Ceballos, Stephanie Dailey, Yongmei Lu, and Tom Grimes, "Social comparisons, social media addiction, and social interaction: An examination of specific social media behaviors related to major depressive disorder in a millennial population," *Journal of Applied Biobehavioral Research* (January 8, 2019).

9   Maryam Mohsin, "10 Social Media Statistics You Need to Know in 2020 [Infographic]," *Oberlo* (August 7, 2020).

10 Esteban Ortiz-Ospina, "The rise of social media," *Our World in Data* (September 18, 2019).

11 Ortiz-Ospina, "The rise of social media."

12 Ortiz-Ospina, "The rise of social media."

13 Ortiz-Ospina, "The rise of social media."

14 "Social Media Fact Sheet," *Pew Research Center: Internet & Technology* (June 12, 2019).

15 Adriana Diaz, "New report links social media use to mental distress in teens," *CBS News* (February 10, 2020).

16 Brian A. Primack, Ariel Shensa, Cesar G. Escobar-Viera, Erica L. Barrett, Jaime E. Sidani, Jason B. Colditz, and A. Everette James, "Use of multiple social media platforms and symptoms of depression and anxiety: A nationally-representative study among U.S. adults," *ScienceDirect* 69 (April 2017): 1–9.

17 Liu yi Lin, Jaime E. Sidani, Ariel Shensa, Ana Radovic, Elizabeth Miller, Jason B. Colditz, Beth L. Hoffman, Leila M. Giles, and Brian A. Primack, "Association between Social Media Use and Depression among U.S. Young Adults," *Depression & Anxiety* (January 19, 2016).

18 "The Diagnostic Criteria for Substance Use Disorders (Addiction)" MentalHelp.net: An American Addiction Centers Resource: *https://www.mentalhelp.net/addiction/diagnostic-criteria*.

19 Daria J. Kuss and Mark D. Griffiths, "Social Networking Sites and Addiction: Ten Lessons Learned," *International Journal of Environmental Research and Public Health* 14(3) (March 17, 2017): 311.

20 Trevor Haynes, "Dopamine, Smartphones & Youth: A battle for your time," *Science in the News*, Harvard University (May 1, 2018).

21 Haynes and Clements, "Dopamine, Smartphones & Youth."

22 "Chamath Palihapitiya, Founder and CEO Social Capital, on Money as an Instrument of Change," Stanford Graduate School of Business (posted November 13, 2017): *https://www.youtube.com/watch?v=PMotykw0SIk*.

23 Taylor Lorenz, "Teens explain the world of Snapchat's addictive streaks, where friendships live or die," *Business Insider* (April 14, 2017).

24 "How the Internet Effects Personal Identity," PSYCH 424 blog, Penn State University (March 16, 2018).

25 Kagan Kircaburun and Mark D. Grffiths, "Problematic Instagram Use: The Role of Perceived Feeling of Presence and Escapism," *International Journal of Mental Health and Addiction* 17 (2019): 909–921.

26 Anna Goldfarb, "Stop Letting Modern Distractions Steal Your Attention," *New York Times* (March 26, 2019).

27 Linda Stone, "FAQ: What is continuous partial attention?" *https://lindastone.net/faq*.

28 Lin, Sidani, et. al., "Association Between Social Media Use and Depression."

29 Nassir Ghaemi, "Snapchat Depression," *Tufts Magazine* (Winter 2019).

30 Paula Durlofsky, "Can Too Much Social Media Cause Depression?" *PsychCentral* (July 8, 2018).

31 Bullying Statistics: *http://www.bullyingstatistics.org/category/bullying-statistics*.

32 Maeve Duggan, "Online Harassment 2017," Pew Research Center: Internet & Technology (July 11, 2017).

33 Elias Aboujaoude, "Cyberbullying: From the Playground to 'Insta,'" *Psychology Today* (January 11, 2015).

34 "5 Different Types of Cyberbullying," End to Cyber Bullying Organization: *www.endcyberbullying.org*.

35 Rebecca Webber, "The Comparison Trap," *Psychology Today* (November 7, 2017).

36 Kalev Leetaru, "Is Social Media Becoming Too Toxic?" *Forbes* (July 19, 2018).

37 Diane Samson, "Poll Declares 'Like' Button As One Of The Most Toxic Social Media Features," *Tech Times* (August 30, 2019).

38 Sherrie Bourg Carter, "Emotions Are Contagious—Choose Your Company Wisely," Psychology Today (October 20, 2012). James H. Fowler and Nicholas A. Christakis, "Dynamic spread of happiness in a large social network: longitudinal analysis over 20 years in the Framingham Heart Study," *The British Medical Journal* (December 5, 2008).

39 Emilio Ferrara and Zeyao Yang, "Measuring Emotional Contagion in Social Media," PLoS ONE 10(11): e0142390 (November 6, 2015).

40 Lynette L. Craft and Frank M. Perna, "The Benefits of Exercise for the Clinically Depressed," *The Primary Care Companion to the Journal of Clinical Psychiatry* 6(3) (2004):104–111.

41 F. Dimeo, M. Bauer, I. Varahram, G. Proest, and U. Halter, "Benefits from aerobic exercise in patients with major depression: a pilot study," *British Journal of Sports Medicine* 35(2).

42 Duke Today Staff, "Study: Exercise Has Long-lasting Effect on Depression," *Duke Today* (September 22, 2000).

43 "Mental Health Information: Major Depression," National Institute of Mental Health: *https://www.nimh.nih.gov/health/statistics/major-depression.shtml*.

44 Lawrence Robinson and Melinda Smith, "Social Media and Mental Health," HelpGuide: *https://www.helpguide.org/articles/mental-health/social-media-and-mental-health*.htm.

45 Jim Taylor, "Technology: Virtual vs. Real Life: You Choose," *Psychology Today* (May 31, 2011).